I0446764

THE HIDDEN FORECLOSURE DEAL MARKET

How to Find a Below-Market Foreclosure Deal

DONNY CORAM

DEDICATION

To God, who gives the strength to know that all things are possible through Him. "I don't feel no-ways tired. I've come too far from where I've started from. Nobody told me the road would be easy. No, I don't believe He brought me this far to leave me" (Rev. James Cleveland).

To my mentors, teachers, coaches, and clients I have met along the way, especially my first real estate coach, Michael Jake, thank you for the guidance and the confidence in my abilities.

To my mom and dad, who always stood by my decisions both good and bad even when they didn't exactly agree with them. Thank you for providing a family structure that always allowed my brothers and me to fail forward fast while still giving us the support and encouragement we needed to flourish. Your accomplishments have not gone unnoticed. I love you both.

To my amazing daughters, Isabella "Izzi," Olivia "Liv-Liv," and Alexandra "Alli-Gator," who have been on this journey with me literally since the day they were born. You have given me purpose when I believed I had none. Thank you for continually making me proud to be your dad. It's still and will always be my favorite job. I love you girls.

And to my beautiful wife, Laura. We did it, babe. From that crazy idea at the rooftop pool in downtown Denver, where we decided to tackle fifty flips in one year.

Although it was a daunting idea, what was truly incredible was the amount of effort we put in to developing the business that made this journey possible. Thank you. You are my queen, my rock, and the love of my life. I will never be able to fully repay you for all you've done for me, but the greatest gift you have ever given me is your love and support (though the Taylor guitar is a close second). Thank you for your ongoing belief in this vision. I hope you always remember how much I adore you. I love you, Laura Coram.

CONTENTS

INTRODUCTION

Since you're taking the time to read this book, I am going to make a couple of basic assumptions about you. You are likely someone who has done some preliminary research on the subject of real estate investing. Maybe you've even acquired an investment property in the past. Perhaps you're trying to start your investment career and you're looking to acquire your first investment property but you aren't sure on how to really get started. Whatever the case, there's a good chance that our paths have crossed because of the word *foreclosure*.

As we start this journey, I'd like you to know that we share something in common already. Since the first free market system was fundamentally defined by economist Adam Smith in *The Wealth of Nations* written in 1776, there has been an ongoing demand for people to want to find a good deal. And based on your existing or developing interest in the real estate investment market, it's a fair bet that you are the type that works to consistently "beat the system" by finding a great deal. I want to first commend you, because the great deal hunters of the market have made record-breaking changes in our economy and our culture.

Imagine where the investment world would be without the great deal hunters. Without the infamous Warren Buffet and his ability to identify opportunities like Apple, Coca-Cola, Paramount, and a slew of other companies, you may not have ever heard of these powerhouse brands. Not to say that these companies couldn't have stood on their own, but that we'll never know for sure.

Jeff Bezos built the Amazon platform on the idea that by removing the brick-and-mortar costs from *every* business, he could provide one-stop shopping, a powerful distribution channel, *and* a better deal on the products he offers on his all-encompassing website.

It is the nature of successful people to want the best value for the smallest investment. Note I didn't say "price." Smart business people want to *invest* their money for the maximum value. In the past four years in the real estate market, there have been a minimal number of foreclosures. But every market changes, and the real estate market of 2022 will be noted by real estate professionals for years from today as a significant turning point in the real estate market. This pivot in the market will lead to the foreclosure market seeing a significant surge in number and potential profit as the market is reset by the financial policymakers that are just now starting to grasp the impact of the red-hot, never-seen-before inflation in the housing market. As the saying goes, "What goes up must come down," and I believe we are going to see the real estate market experience a notable downturn. Why? Because all markets are cyclical, and the real estate market of 2023 is well past its cyclical norms based on any analysis of readily available real estate data. In my professional opinion, a foreclosure market is imminent, unavoidable, and, yes, *favorable* to educated investors who understand market cycles and are prepared to capitalize on the new market norms. The foreclosure market is coming, and large-scale investors, including hedge funds, are preparing for the foreclosure crisis.

Most people know that knowledge is power. This book is intended to provide you with some initial knowledge about where to look for these hidden foreclosure deals and then provide you with my 5-step process to turn these opportunities into a consistent source of income for you and your family. The process I will show you in this book will help you analyze property, fund it with other people's money, hire a construction team to fix it to salable condition, and flip it for a profit of $25,000 or more by reducing your transaction costs.

The foreclosure market is much harder to access and analyze than the retail real estate market. As a professional real estate investment business coach, podcast host, and fellow investor, my goal for this book is to pique your interest in foreclosure investing by teaching you how I used some specific tools and tactics to find these foreclosure deals, acquire them, fix them to market, and resell them at a substantial profit in the red-hot markets of 2020–2021. Once you know where and how to look for these deals, my hope is you will use this knowledge to find some great foreclosure deals in your market. I also hope that once you are exposed to this hidden foreclosure deals market, you will then begin to look to find a system of education and accountability through professional real estate investment coaching, ideally through my coaching program.

I am certain that the knowledge you will gain from this book will help you build your portfolio, create and or increase your passive cash flow, and make a significant profit on these "hidden" foreclosure deals using my cutting-edge 5 F's of Foreclosure Investment System, which you can learn more about here:

www.foreclosuredealscoach.com/5fis.

However, before you make an investment in any investment course, you're looking to learn the basics, so let's dive in and learn a little more about what a foreclosure is and why they are such great deals for the real estate investor who understands how to consistently find these deals, sell them at a profit, or keep them in their portfolio for passive income and long term appreciation.

CHAPTER 1

WHO AM I?

A question you may have before we start this book is, who am I, and why should you take *any* advice from me, much less advice on investing in one of the most expensive asset classes available, real estate?

Well, you certainly didn't buy this book to learn more about me, so I'll keep this short and sweet. In December of 2007, I found myself working for a tech company in the support department in Colorado Springs, Colorado. As is typical for a December morning, the steep driveway of my suburban home was coated in a sheet of black ice covered by an innocent-looking layer of snow.

As I hurriedly prepared for another mundane day at the office, a sudden slip on the icy surface sent me tumbling to the ground. The unfortunate fall resulted in an injured ankle and an overwhelming mix of pain and relief—pain from the throbbing ankle, but relief from the sudden realization that I wouldn't be able to make it to work that day.

With a mixture of groans and sighs, I limped back into the house, contemplating the unexpected day off. Little did I know that this seemingly unfortunate incident would become the turning point in my life.

As I spent the day resting and nursing my ankle, I couldn't help but reflect on my current job and life choices. The injury had forced me to slow down, providing the rare opportunity to reassess my priorities and dreams. Hours turned into days, and during this unexpected break, I stumbled upon the world of real estate investing.

Fueled by newfound curiosity and the desire for financial freedom, I delved into real estate books, online courses, and networking events. The injury, initially perceived as a setback, became the catalyst for a profound change in perspective. The more I learned about real estate investing, the more passionate and excited I became.

Soon, I started attending local real estate meetups, connecting with seasoned investors and absorbing knowledge like a sponge. The injury, which had confined me to my home, turned into an opportunity to build a new path for my future.

As my ankle healed, I made the bold decision to transition away from the unfulfilling job and pursue a career in real estate investing full time. I began by purchasing my first fix-and-flip property, leveraging the newfound knowledge and networking connections I had acquired. Despite making nearly every mistake a newbie investor can make, I managed to walk away from that first deal with a $17,846.32 profit, which represented about a third of the annual income I was making from the day job I hated.

In an act of defiance against the job I had learned to despise, I began to decorate the walls of my office with the checks from each of the deals I had completed. I proudly announced to my coworkers that once the copies of checks completed a full line from one side of my cubicle prison to the other, I would quit my job. My passion for finding great deals combined with making a significant investment in a real estate coaching program allowed me to make progress in my cubicle real estate check display very quickly. As the mural of checks on my office wall hit roughly 75 percent to my goal, I was called into the HR office of my employer. The HR administrator, who I had a really good relationship with, invited me into her office and asked me to take a seat. I hesitated at first but eventually took a seat in her plush office guest chair.

She straightened her glasses, which I immediately recognized as a sign that this wasn't going to be good news.

"How are you, Donny?" she politely asked.

Clearly annoyed, I responded, "I'm fine, Amy, can we get to the point please? What's up?"

She ignored my flippant attitude, a skill she had mastered over a couple of years of dealing with me. "Okay, I'll get to it, Your checks are becoming a problem for morale, and we're going to need you to take them down."

I thought to myself, "Well, that's not going to happen," but thought better of saying it out loud, as Amy had always been professional and nice to me. Instead I pretended to be ignorant and asked, "How could pictures of checks be a problem for employee morale?"

Amy gathered her thoughts for a moment and then responded in her very condescending HR voice, "Donny, I think you know the problem. People are stopping by your cube and seeing that you are making substantially more from your real estate investment deals than you do from your employment here. Now management is starting to question why you work here at all. The bottom line is I have an official request from upper management to take the check pictures down immediately, because many consider them offensive."

"In that case," I quickly snapped back, "I have decided that I find pictures of people's children offensive, so if I have to take my checks down, then I think the other employees should have to take their kid pictures down too." I knew I was being ridiculous, but I also felt hurt and betrayed that my journey to success through real estate was considered offensive to the "crabs in a bucket" I shared office space with every day.

"Now you're just being silly, Donny. Listen, I went to bat for you on this already, but management isn't going to budge here, so you either go out there and take the checks down or . . ."

"Or *what?*" I inquired.

"Or I've been instructed to terminate your employment here effective immediately. This package will explain how your termination will work." She pushed over a folder. I snatched the package from her desk, opened it, quickly signed it, and slid it back to her.

"Amy, I appreciate you going to bat for me, but this is too far for me." She nodded in acknowledgment, picked up the document, and extended her hand. "It's been fun working with you. Good luck with the real estate thing. I hope it works out for you." I could sense the doubt in her voice. I was fuming with anger but did my best to compose myself, thanked her for her time, and walked out the door.

As I began to pack my things, a voice from the other side of the cubicle wall, my good friend and my partner on my first flip deal, said, "Good luck, man, and leave the check pictures. If they want them down so badly, make them take them down." I agreed, high-fived him, grabbed my box of things, and walked out the door.

Upon arrival home, I broke down in tears. I had never been fired from a job like that before. I felt like I had let my family down by losing my job. Despite my success in real estate, I was terrified of losing the stable paycheck I had relied on throughout my career. Sure, I had always had a side hustle of some kind, but could I really do real estate investing full time and provide for my young family? After recounting the story to my wife, she sat me down and told me, "It's probably the best thing that ever happened to you. You hated that job; now get to work." Revitalized by her support, I took a deep breath and began to assess what I already had going for me. I was passionate about real estate and was already making more from my real estate business than I was from my day job and loved the industry. I also knew how to find great deals in the market, and evaluating hundreds of deals had given me a lot of experience in deal analysis.

Having found the courage I needed, I looked down, picked up my phone, and called my real estate investment coach, Mike.

"Finally!" he exclaimed. "You didn't belong there anyway. Now let's get to work."

Over time, my real estate portfolio grew, and with each successful investment, I gained more confidence and financial stability. What started as a slip on the icy driveway, leading to an ankle injury, transformed into the stepping stone for a fulfilling and prosperous career in real estate.

As I look back on that fateful day, I can't help but marvel at the unexpected turn of events. The slip on the driveway, initially seen as a stroke of misfortune, had become the catalyst for a journey toward a more meaningful and rewarding life. And so, my story became an inspiring tale of resilience, adaptability, and the transformative power of unexpected opportunities. I hope that you don't have to injure yourself to realize your true calling in life. If it's real estate investing, I would be honored to be one of your guides to help you alter the course of your life, and if your passions lie elsewhere, it is my sincere desire to help you learn how to use real estate investing to build the additional income and wealth you need to pursue that passion, no matter what it is.

Now that you know my journey into real estate investing, let's talk about my favorite real estate investment vehicle: foreclosure investing. While there are unlimited ways to build income and wealth with real estate, the foreclosure real estate market has quickly become my favorite. With my increasing transaction count, I have learned a unique skill for communicating and negotiating with banks, government entities, and local agents in the foreclosure market.

CHAPTER 2

WHAT IS A FORECLOSURE?

When a bank repossesses a property, it is commonly known as a *foreclosure*. A little further thought tells you three things about these foreclosures.:

1. You probably understand that when a bank or the federal government forecloses on a property, it is not something they *want* to do. The feds and banks are not in the housing business. They are in the *money* business, which means they don't *want* the property. This, by definition, makes them motivated sellers.

2. If the homeowner couldn't or didn't sell a property on the retail market, it probably means the property is in below retail condition. This generally means there is significant deferred maintenance or perhaps even extensive damage to the property.

3. If you could just *find* a few of these foreclosed properties, fix the problems with them, and bring them back to retail condition, you could make a profit by investing money in these below-market properties currently held by motivated sellers.

The problem most of my coaching clients face during our first meeting is how to find these foreclosure and distressed properties. After all, you can't make a profit buying a house at or above market price, right? Buying low and selling high is still a great way to make money in any market. However, due to the added complication involved in finding the best deals on real estate investment properties, the profit potential of finding foreclosure deals makes it very lucrative for investors who know where to look for these properties and acquire them before other savvy investors do.

This book will help real estate investors locate the inside sources where foreclosure deals can be found and acquired. Though I refer to this as the "hidden real estate market," once you understand how to access these sources, you will realize that the best deals in your real estate market are actually hiding in plain sight. My goal is to give you the knowledge I have used to find the hundreds of distressed properties I have flipped over the past twelve years. By the end of this book, you will understand one of the most important steps in the foreclosure deal location process. Once you understand how to locate properties in this hidden market, I promise that you will never look at the real estate market the same way again. You will understand the path to consistently finding below-market deals and thus fuel your real estate business and portfolio to grow faster with a substantially higher rate of return than buying market-priced properties.

Look, I'm not going to give you some "get rich quick" scheme to make millions in foreclosure investing overnight. Many "gurus" out there would have you believe otherwise, but there is no actual shortcut to building wealth in real estate. Instead, the market offers those who are willing to put in a little extra effort in education to find the best deals in the market. What I *will* teach you in the next few chapters are real-world solutions that address these three key points:

1. The best online sources for government-owned foreclosed properties – These are the sites I regularly use to find some of the best foreclosure deals available in your market.

2. Off-market strategies to re-route the best deals directly to your inbox and FB messenger.

3. The mental game - How to approach each of these sources to ensure you can get the best deal possible by negotiating with foreclosing institutions, both banks and the government. This understanding helps to ensure that your offer gets the attention it needs to be accepted consistently.

So why should you take my advice? The first step to answering that question is to explain where I am coming from and how I started investing in foreclosures. Over the past fifteen years, my team and I have completed hundreds of fixes and flips on bank- and government-owned foreclosures. To gain the knowledge I needed to be a successful foreclosure investor, I attended hundreds of hours of real estate meetups, read countless books on real estate investing, spent $100,000 or more on seminars and real estate conferences all over the country, and met and worked with some of the greatest minds in the foreclosure industry. I have put this to work—not in theory, but in the real world. I have used my boots on the ground and real-world experience to bring deals from concept to completion. Along the journey, I've heard the nos, learned what works and what doesn't, and learned how to make a deal that doesn't work into one that does. In the end, I have become one of the most successful foreclosure investors in the country by accomplishing the following goals:

- Successfully completing forty-seven fix and flips in 2021
- Gaining national recognition for a flip we completed. Search #springshellhouse for some scary before/after pics and news stories
- Obtaining over $1 million in equity on rental property I have acquired from foreclosure
- Creating and managing an operations team that allows me the freedom to continue my projects from anywhere in the world
- Using my experience to attract private lenders who are willing to fund 100 percent of the capital needed for my fix-and-flip projects

I want you to know all of that because I obtained my education in foreclosure investing the hard way. And while I can't teach you everything you need to know to master the investment market in one short e-book, I can help you reduce and eliminate some of the mistakes that seem obvious to me now. By applying some of the principles and sources I will share with you, you can improve your life through real estate investing. I pride myself on having the heart of a teacher. If you share my passion for the real estate business and want to learn a skill that can and will provide generational wealth to you and your family, let's dive in.

Looking a Little Closer

Do you think you can gain the knowledge you need to be a pilot by watching a pilot land a plane? If your friend obtained their knowledge of aviation from watching YouTube Pilot Training (is that even a thing?), would you willingly hop on a plane with him or her? Obviously not. Unfortunately, the world's real estate "gurus" have created a very lucrative industry for themselves by convincing very educated people that they can learn real estate investing by reading their latest book or spending tens of thousands of dollars on a course. The truth is, many mental gymnastics are constantly taking place in the mind of a successful real estate investor. The true discipline required to learn this process takes time to master, like any other useful skill. Yet I meet many people who think they can read a series of books and succeed in real estate. Like any skill, this is best learned over time and with full immersion into the craft. Dabbling in real estate will yield results, but mastery takes dedication. And dedication requires a time investment. Thankfully, the online education space is providing people the opportunity to utilize the knowledge that others have obtained over decades of experience by simply taking an online course. While this is not a complete substitute for direct experience, the abundance of available information has made it a close second.

As an example, LeBron James just became the first billionaire who is still currently playing the sport of basketball. I've had the pleasure of watching King James play in person from courtside seats, and I can tell you I learned nothing about how he has dominated the world of basketball and business from my observations from the bleachers. However, as I've looked closer at LeBron's career, I can tell you that he followed some key steps that can be applied to any successful endeavor:

- Study the real estate market as a whole, not just the subsection of foreclosures.
- Assemble a team of data-fed expert advisors. (Never take advice from those who trade on emotion.)
- Take substantial action to apply what you have learned.

Studying the Market

The real estate market operates in several subsections. The first and most utilized is the *retail market*. The retail market provides a consistently changing guide to what the market is willing to pay for properties. Many investors try to ignore the retail market to their own peril because it seems less interesting than the deals market. The saying I am constantly offering to my students is, "You make your money on real estate when you *buy* it; you realize that gain when the property is sold." There are multiple factors that go into a successful acquisition. While sourcing your properties to provide a consistent deal flow is important, there are multiple factors, including funding, minimizing your repair budget, and market competition, that go into a successful foreclosure deal acquisition.

This is before the pressing issues regarding the funding and sales processes that can make even the best acquisition less profitable. Therefore, the best real estate coaches slow the process down for their students. By forcing the student to focus on what stage they are in, the coach can break down each factor of a foreclosure deal acquisition to make the buying process easier and more consistent.

The Reverse Flip Process

Start with the end in mind.

—Stephen Covey

One of my favorite things to do is to show my coaching students a breakdown of my successful flips in reverse. Basically, I start with the pictures of or a visit to the completed property and follow each of the steps I took in reverse to allow my coaching students to "experience" each step of the fix-and-flip process. I start with the profit at the end of the deal and ultimately end with the source of the acquisition.

This full reverse analysis with a newbie investor usually gives them the clarity they are looking for. One of my favorite parts of being a business coach is seeing my students' eyes light up when they realize that there are profitable foreclosure opportunities all around them. The sheer number of moving parts in a foreclosure deal acquisition seems overwhelming, but when a source of deals is presented and coupled with the knowledge to complete those deals, the very difficult becomes very easy.

Finding deals in any market seems daunting to most newbies, and it can be a difficult process. However, once you understand the psychology of lending institutions and know where to look for foreclosure deals, you will have the confidence you need to build a business that consistently **finds** great deals, **figures** out their fair market value, **funds** deals using investor money sources, **fixes** the deals to market, and then **flips** those deals on the market for a profit. To learn more about these steps, check out my 5 F's of Foreclosure Investment System at www.foreclosuredealscoach.com/5fis.

HUD Foreclosures

One of my favorite sources of deals are HUD foreclosures, but before I dive into why HUD foreclosures are such great deals, let's discuss what a HUD foreclosure is.

In the realm of real estate, the term *HUD foreclosure* refers to a property that was once financed with a Federal Housing Administration (FHA) loan and has subsequently gone through the foreclosure process. The US Department of Housing and Urban Development (HUD) plays a crucial role in managing and selling these foreclosed properties. This process has its own unique characteristics, procedures, and opportunities for potential buyers.

Origin and Purpose of FHA Loans

HUD foreclosures typically stem from properties financed with FHA loans. FHA loans are mortgages insured by the Federal Housing Administration, a division of HUD. These loans are designed to make homeownership more accessible by providing lenders with insurance against potential borrower defaults. However, when a borrower defaults on an FHA-insured loan, the property becomes the responsibility of HUD.

While it is a common misconception that the FHA is a lender, it is important to understand that the FHA is, in fact, a government-backed insurance company that was created to promote homeownership by allowing for reduced down payment programs aimed to help first-time homebuyers. As of this writing, the FHA down payment is 3.5 percent which is a significant difference from the 20 percent that is often required by conventional lenders.

The Federal Housing Administration (FHA) was created in 1934 as part of the National Housing Act during the Great Depression. The primary objective was to address the housing crisis by providing a stable and affordable mortgage market. At the time, the private mortgage market was struggling, making it difficult for many Americans to secure home loans.

The FHA's original mission was to stimulate the housing industry, increase employment, and facilitate home ownership by insuring mortgages. The agency aimed to make homeownership more accessible, especially for those who faced challenges in obtaining traditional loans, such as low-income individuals and first-time homebuyers.

One of the key mechanisms introduced by the FHA was mortgage insurance. The agency offered lenders insurance on mortgages for qualifying borrowers, mitigating the risk of default.

This innovation made lenders more willing to provide loans to a broader range of borrowers, as they were protected against potential losses.

The FHA has played a vital role in making homeownership attainable for first-time buyers. By providing mortgage insurance, the FHA lowered the down payment requirements for borrowers, making it more feasible for individuals with limited financial resources to enter the housing market. The agency's programs have been particularly beneficial for those who may not meet the stringent criteria set by private lenders.

Another significant contribution of the FHA was the introduction of the 30-year fixed-rate mortgage. This mortgage structure offered borrowers a stable and predictable payment plan, making homeownership more sustainable over the long term. The 30-year fixed-rate mortgage became a standard in the industry, providing stability and affordability for countless homeowners, including many first-time buyers.

After World War II, the FHA played a pivotal role in facilitating the post-war housing boom. The agency insured millions of mortgages, helping returning veterans and their families achieve the American dream of homeownership. This period saw a substantial increase in suburban development and a surge in the number of families owning their own homes.

Over the years, the FHA has evolved and adapted its programs to meet the changing needs of the housing market. The agency has introduced various initiatives, including energy-efficient mortgage programs and down payment assistance programs, to continue supporting first-time homebuyers and underserved communities.

Today, the FHA continues to assist first-time homebuyers through a range of programs. These programs include low down payment requirements, flexible credit standards, and government-backed insurance, making it easier for individuals with limited financial resources to qualify for mortgages.

The FHA has played a crucial role in the history of homeownership in the United States. By introducing innovative programs and mortgage insurance, the FHA has helped millions of first-time homebuyers overcome financial barriers and achieve the dream of owning a home, contributing significantly to the stability and growth of the American housing market.

However, like every government program, the FHA has some significant flaws. By providing lower down payment programs, the FHA allows people who may not be as financially stable to achieve the dream of owning a home. As a result, many of these borrowers find themselves in situations where they can no longer afford the payments on their mortgages. When an FHA borrower defaults on their mortgage, it goes through the same foreclosure process as other types of mortgages, with one notable difference. During the process, instead of the foreclosing property going to the lender, the FHA pays the lender for the default amount, and the house is deeded to the US Federal Government's Department of Housing and Urban Development (HUD), and it becomes what we as investors know as a HUD home.

While your first encounter with a HUD home will likely be after the property has foreclosed, the current market conditions may put you in a situation where the property is going through the foreclosure process. For this reason, it's important for you to have some understanding of the HUD foreclosure process.

The Foreclosure Process

When a homeowner with an FHA loan fails to meet their mortgage obligations, the lender initiates foreclosure proceedings. Upon completion of the foreclosure process, which may include legal proceedings and auctions, the property is repossessed by the lender, and ownership is transferred to HUD. HUD then becomes the seller of the foreclosed property.

HUD-Owned Properties

HUD's inventory of foreclosed homes then becomes available for purchase to the public. These properties vary widely in terms of size, condition, and location. Interested buyers can find a diverse range of options, from single-family homes to multi-unit dwellings, across various neighborhoods and communities.

The HUDHomeStore.com

HUD manages the sale of its foreclosed properties through the HUDHomeStore.com, an online platform that allows potential buyers to search for available properties and submit offers.

The website provides detailed information about each property, including its condition, its features, and the necessary steps for purchase.

Exclusive Listing Periods

To promote owner-occupancy, HUD establishes exclusive listing periods during which only potential owner-occupant buyers can submit offers. Investors and other buyers are allowed to bid on these properties only after the exclusive period expires. This is an important feature of the HUD process for investors to understand, as there are two phases of the HUD foreclosure listing periods that are important to you as an investor: the exclusive listing period and the extended listing period.

The HUD foreclosure exclusive listing period is a specific timeframe during which only owner-occupant buyers have the opportunity to submit offers on HUD-owned properties. This period is designed to prioritize individuals who intend to live in the property as their primary residence, promoting the goal of increasing homeownership in communities. Here are the key aspects of the HUD foreclosure exclusive listing period:

1) Purpose: The primary purpose of the exclusive listing period is to encourage owner-occupancy. HUD aims to give individuals and families looking for a home to live in an advantage over investors or buyers looking for properties solely for investment purposes. This helps in fostering stable communities and neighborhoods by ensuring that properties are purchased by those who plan to reside in them.

2) Duration: The length of the exclusive listing period can vary. Typically, it lasts for an initial period, often around ten to fifteen days, during which only bids from owner-occupant buyers are considered. In recent years, many markets, including mine, have extended this period to up to thirty days. After this exclusive period, the property becomes available for bids from all potential buyers, including investors.

3) Definition of *owner-occupant*: HUD defines an owner-occupant as someone who will make the purchased property their primary residence within a specific timeframe, usually within sixty days after closing the sale. This ensures that individuals genuinely interested in living in the property have the opportunity to participate in the exclusive listing period. There can be severe penalties for violating this and attempting to flip a HUD foreclosure purchased during the exclusive listing period. These penalties can include up to a $250,000 fine, and some documents even suggest jail time. While I am often asked by investors about these penalties, my response is generally the same: it's not worth it. There are typically plenty of opportunities to buy HUD foreclosures as an investor, so it is best to follow this rule.

4) Bidding process during the exclusive period: During the exclusive listing period, owner-occupant buyers can submit their bids through a HUD-registered real estate broker. Bids are evaluated based on various factors, including the offered price, financing method, and buyer's intention to occupy the property. Regardless of the buying period, bids for owner-occupant buyers will be given preference, so in a competitive market, you can lose a HUD bid to an owner-occupant even if you are the highest bidder on the property.

5) Competitive advantage: Owner-occupant buyers often have a competitive advantage during this exclusive period. If multiple bids are submitted, HUD may prioritize the bid that offers the highest price and demonstrates a commitment to occupying the property. This can give families and individuals seeking a home to live in an edge over investors who may be looking for properties purely for rental or resale purposes.

6) Investor participation after exclusive period: Once the exclusive listing period concludes, the property becomes available for bids from all potential buyers, including investors. This phase opens up the opportunity for a broader pool of buyers to participate in the bidding process. This period is known as the extended period, and we will cover it a little later on in this book.

7) Affordability and community stability: By encouraging owner-occupancy, the exclusive listing period aligns with HUD's broader goals of promoting affordable housing and fostering stable communities. When properties are purchased by individuals who plan to live in them, it contributes to the stability and vitality of neighborhoods. The bottom line is that HUD would prefer that HUD homes go to owner-occupant bidders. However, many HUD homes are in a condition that simply makes them a better fit for real estate investors.

The HUD foreclosure exclusive listing period is a strategic initiative to prioritize and support owner-occupant buyers during the early stages of the property sale process. This approach aligns with HUD's mission to expand homeownership opportunities and create thriving communities.

Financing and Repairs

HUD homes are sold "as is," and potential buyers should be prepared for the possibility of needed repairs. However, HUD offers special financing options, such as the FHA 203(k) loan, which allows buyers to include repair costs in the mortgage. This feature can be particularly attractive to buyers looking to invest in properties that may require rehabilitation. HUD homes provide a great opportunity for investment-minded owner-occupant buyers to build sweat equity. However, with higher interest rates in recent years, most retail homebuyers are not willing to pay a higher mortgage payment *and* have to put money in their home. For this reason, many more HUD homes are not selling in the exclusive period, which is providing opportunities for real estate investors to buy and remodel these homes for a profit.

Bidding and Winning

Bidding on a HUD foreclosure involves submitting an offer through a HUD-registered real estate broker. This has also become a problem because the recent surge of people getting their real estate license to capitalize on the low-interest market, coupled with the low inventory of HUD homes in recent years, means that the majority of agents do not get registered to sell HUD homes. My coaching program works with agents all over the country who are registered to sell HUDs, but HUD agents can be hard to find.

The bids on HUD homes are evaluated based on various factors, including the offered price, the financing method, and whether the buyer intends to occupy the property. The highest and most acceptable bid is then selected.

Potential for Savings

One of the key advantages of purchasing a HUD foreclosure is the potential for savings. These properties are often priced below market value, making them an attractive option for first-time homebuyers, real estate investors, and those looking for affordable housing opportunities.

In conclusion, HUD foreclosures present a unique avenue for acquiring real estate with the potential for significant savings. Understanding the process, being aware of the unique features of HUD-owned properties, and navigating the HUDHomestore.com website are essential steps for individuals interested in exploring this segment of the real estate market.

CHAPTER 3

THE BEST SOURCES OF DEALS

In the last chapter, we briefly talked about the HUD Homestore as a resource for finding foreclosed homes, and thus deals you can take advantage of as an investor. In this section, we will talk about HUD Homestore more in-depth, as well as several other great sources of deals.

Source #1: The MLS

I would be extremely wealthy if I had a dollar for every time I was told by would-be real estate investors and agents that there are no deals on the market. When notorious bank robber Willie Sutton, was asked why he robbed banks, his reply was, "Because that's where the money is." Well, in our case, the MLS is where the money is, because that's where the houses are.

The MLS or *multiple listing service* is a database of all properties for sale, under contract, pending sale, and sold in your local market. While the most common way to access the MLS is to obtain a real estate agent license, in recent years, several software companies, including Privy, have offered and provided real estate data to unlicensed people. To check out how Privy can help you find foreclosures and other distressed property deals in your local market, use my affiliate link for Privy (www.fdcprivy.com) to start an account, and then schedule a call with me for a free Deal-Finding Session where we'll use this tool to find great below-market listings in your area: www.foreclosuredealscoach.com.

Though the crazy-hyped real estate market would have you believe otherwise, I consistently find great deals on the MLS. Though many are foreclosures, the inflated real estate market has allowed retail sellers to list properties in need of significant rehab at significantly below-market prices. One of my recent on-market acquisitions was a pre-foreclosure we purchased for $1,050,000 and resold for nearly $1,400,000. I learned about this property from one of my favorite sources, a real estate agent, who I formed a relationship with over six years before they brought me this deal.

So why is there an overwhelming myth that there are no deals on the market? Well, part of the psychology you need to understand about foreclosure acquisition is that the best deals in the market do not last very long. If you are looking at the MLS weekly, you are limiting yourself to a one-in-seven chance of finding a deal on the market that day. The best deals on the market last for hours, not days. We have successfully secured foreclosure deals that were on the market for less than six hours before we got the property under contract. How do you stand out when your competitive investor "piranhas" bite at anything in blood-filled water? Again, the best deals do not last long, so think fast. If you want to find the best deals, you must take a look at your MLS system daily or use a tool like Privy to scour the market for you daily and send you the best deals. To sign up for Privy, again, please use my affiliate link: www.fdcprivy.com.

Using Privy or the MLS, if you have access, you can program artificial intelligence systems with your market-specific parameters and receive automated listing notifications from your market every morning. Imagine waking up in the morning to find the best deals on the market in your email. The key is having a consistent stream of relative real estate data being sent to you in as close to real-time as possible. Can you imagine a successful stock trader who checked the market once a week? Of course not. The stock market is far too dynamic for that. The same can be said for the real estate market as it relates to finding great deals. Depending on your local market, location, and price range, retail listings may be on the market for seven days to up to thirty days. However, the foreclosure deals market only operates at one speed, and that speed is *fast*.

Now What?

Do you need proof? If you can access your MLS or Privy, pick a zip code you are familiar with. Our first objective is to determine the average price per square foot in that zip code. For the sake of this exercise, I'm going to use Colorado Springs zip code 80916, one of my favorite zip codes to find foreclosure deals in, largely because of its lower price point.

Right now, the average price per square foot in this zip code is $240. Generally speaking, we are looking to buy distressed properties from motivated sellers for 70–80 percent of their retail value. In this case, that would mean buying the property for $168–$192 a square foot.

While this is a general starting point, my goal is to show you just how often deals hit the market and then demonstrate the limited time frame these deals are available.

A quick search on the sold data shows just over 120 single-family home listings that sold in the past ninety days in this zip code at $192 a square foot or less. Further analysis shows the average number of days on the market is three. While this seems to suggest that you have seventy-two hours to find deals in this space, as a former licensed agent, I can tell you that there is generally a delay of a day or even two between a property going under contract and the necessary status update on the MLS. Most successful agents are very busy, so changing the status of a property is generally not a high priority. As a result, this data is heavily skewed by the human element of delay. A conversation with many of the listing agents who had deals in this zip code would yield an actual time on the market that would be better measured in hours, not days. I can say with certainty that the best deals I have acquired on the market are under contract in twenty-four hours or less from activating the listing on the market.

Don't get me wrong, the MLS is still a great source of deals for active real estate investors, but the early bird definitely gets the worm. Remember that agents are people, and as people they have lives. Many agents, like me, need quiet time late in the evening to get their listings entered into and activated on the MLS. As such, the best time to find deals is in the morning. Start your day before the rest of the market does, set showings as early as possible, and prepare and submit your "hassle-free offer" to the lending institutions as early as possible. Doing so will provide you with a consistent stream of foreclosure deals from the most obvious source, the MLS.

Once you've located a well-priced deal, do your homework *before* going to see the property. This way, you are prepared to submit an offer in the field. I have acquired countless market deals by being more prepared than my competition. Banks prefer to deal with buyers who can make swift decisions. I have watched competitive investors scramble to do their market analysis while I have already prepared my offer and submitted it. In the Colorado Springs market, for example, there are over five thousand licensed real estate agents at the time of writing this book. That's five thousand potential competitors who may have multiple investor buyers interested in a foreclosed property that is just hitting the market. Though only a small percentage of these buyers are looking to buy a deal, that percentage fluctuates based on market inventory. As inventory rises, the home-buying market will increasingly look for opportunities in that market. The shortage of inventory over the past few years has created a market "impression" that there are no deals. The reality is that there *are* fewer deals currently available. The other reality is that we are witnessing a significant market shift. During this shift, deals will be plentiful, but only experienced operators will have the fortitude and funding to take on those deals. By getting educated about the hidden foreclosure market now, you are taking the first steps toward preparing for the abundance of real estate investment opportunities the market offers the educated and confident investor.

Right now, I want you to take a moment to dispel the myth in your head that there are no deals on the MLS. There are most certainly deals in every market.

The MLS tracks Days on Market (DOM), not hours on market. As such, there's a false perception that you have several days to pursue under-market opportunities. If the market showed the correct data, you would understand that the best deals last hours. If you want to obtain foreclosure deals on the MLS, you must start early, research before you see the property, and submit your hassle-free offer quickly to have a chance of acquiring these deals. In the recent years of a very competitive real estate market, many agents have learned to pursue only the low-hanging fruit in the real estate market. While this benefits both the agent and the retail buyer, it offers little value to the investor who is looking for a deal. Now that you know you *can* find deals on the market, I encourage you to find a way to look at your target market consistently and with increased awareness. Your ability to buy deals in a competitive market will be an important factor in the determination of the return on investment in your portfolio. So look early and look often.

Source #2 - Government and Bank Foreclosure Websites

www.hudhomestore.com

I obtained my real estate license in 2007. In 2008, the United States economy was in the middle of one of the biggest recessions in American history. The recession was largely considered to be caused by the collapse of the housing market due to the overgrowth of the sub-prime lending industry. During this time, the federal government was overwhelmed with FHA loans, which were typically offered to first-time homebuyers due to their low downpayment requirements. When these government-backed loans failed to perform, the government came into possession of tens of thousands of foreclosed properties. In order to recover the capital, the Department of Housing and Urban Development quickly created a web-based resource to allow for the quick sale of what became known as HUD foreclosures. While this was a very difficult time for those who lost their home, it proved to be an excellent time for investor-focused agents like me to sell those foreclosures to investors. I believe that we are at the edge of a similar market right now.

Although I started my real estate career on the investing side, the quick change in the economy in 2008, coupled with the birth of my second daughter, forced me to give up my real estate investment career temporarily, and I went back into the workforce against my will. I decided that my time as an investor would have to be put on hold until I had enough money to support my family.

However, I knew that the knowledge I had obtained in the foreclosure investment space would be valuable to other investors. This knowledge quickly propelled me to be the state's top HUD foreclosure agent. However, it drove me nearly insane to know I couldn't buy the incredible deals hitting the market. Due to the overwhelming supply of HUD foreclosures, the FHA decided it was wise to incentivize buyers agents to sell their properties. To do so, they offered buyers agents on HUD properties a 5 percent commission on the sale of the homes.

The ability to find deals for my investor clients made selling HUD properties a no-brainer for me. Not only did I love looking at deals in the market, but I was also able to make nearly double the standard 3 percent commission offered on typical homes. The combination of my passion for finding deals and the increased financial incentive to sell those properties made selling HUDs a very lucrative and fulfilling business model. I quickly modernized my marketing methods and created a website, Colorado Foreclosure Deals, and a YouTube channel. I began broadcasting the best deals in the market to would-be investors all across the country using YouTube and Facebook Live Videos, where I would invite viewers to tour the HUD properties with me.

Everyone wants a deal, so this one-stop shop for deal-hunters was a dream come true.

One important thing to note when dealing with the federal government is that they are very inefficient and unorganized. Though in 2008, they had reason to feel overwhelmed, and even today, the process of buying a HUD foreclosure is cumbersome at best. Couple that with the fact that most markets have had few foreclosures in recent years, and what you have is a relatively untapped resource to find deals from a very motivated seller, our rich Uncle Sam.

Because of the differences in buying a HUD foreclosure coupled with the scarcity of foreclosure inventory, it is safe to say that most real estate agents have limited or no experience in buying HUD homes. While the homes are supposed to be listed on the market with other homes, I have purchased several homes on the HUD site that should have been listed on the local MLS but were listed in other MLS systems or, in one case, not listed at all.

Since most agents have little to no experience with HUD foreclosures, the HUDHomeStore.gov website can be an excellent place to find opportunities when there are not a lot of foreclosures on the market.

At the time of this writing, there is only 1 HUD foreclosure available in the State of Colorado in a city I've never heard of. While this is disappointing in my home state, there are several states in the country that have twenty or more HUD homes in inventory all the time. While this may seem like too few to be useful, these HUD homes are priced below market by design, and when the market weakens in the next few years, there will be substantially more HUD homes coming.

The HUDHomestore.gov site uses a very predictable pricing model to sell homes. First, the houses on the site are evaluated for market price and then are discounted to 10 percent below what HUD believes the market price to be. While this seems simple enough, it's important to remember that the Department of Housing and Development is a very large government agency trying to play in local markets across the country. As such, their opinion of the value of their property can be and is often wildly inaccurate.

This is an advantage to savvy investors. I have scored some incredible deals on HUD listings that were priced incorrectly. The key is understanding the core mentality that drives HUD to do what they do. It's important to remember that, unlike a traditional seller, HUD properties are a hassle and a burden to the federal government. Once the property is transferred to the custodianship of HUD, they have to take several steps to get the property ready to sell. If you have any experience dealing with the government, you know that they do not tend to move quickly or efficiently. Many HUD properties sit for a year or more before HUD even starts their process. When there were a ton of foreclosures in 2008–2011, this delay in the process meant that many homes suffered from water damage from busted pipes, vandalism, and a variety of other problems associated with vacant properties. As a successful foreclosure specialist, I saw the state of the HUD process during this era. HUD learned the hard way that they were not equipped to manage the properties they now owned. In essence, HUD became the ultimate motivated yet unequipped seller.

This is important information for real estate investors because once you gain an understanding of any seller's motivation, you are far more equipped to utilize that motivation to get a good deal on the property. HUD's primary goal is to recover as much money as they can that was lost in the insurance of the FHA loan that defaulted. They know very little about the property, and because they are a large government agency, not a traditional seller, they have absolutely no emotional attachment to the property or the number of the ultimate sales price.

Their goal is to offload the property quickly to avoid further losses on the property.

HUD Bidding Process

The HUD bidding process is substantially different from a retail offer. The first step is to locate a HUD-registered real estate agent. A HUD-registered agent is required to bid on a HUD property. To prevent additional liability for the feds, HUD will not work with you directly as a buyer. To find a list of HUD-registered brokers in your city, use the search tool below:

https://www.hudhomestore.gov/Listing/BrokerSearch.aspx.

If your preferred agent isn't registered with HUD, which is not uncommon due to the lack of HUD inventory in the current market, you can suggest that your preferred agent get registered with HUD to submit your bid. This process is free, but it does take time. As such, it's crucial to have a HUD-registered agent on your team as soon as possible. I can tell you that as an agent, I did several HUD property acquisitions from people who were in the spheres of very tenured agents in town simply because I was registered and ready to go, and the agent couldn't register in time to submit a bid before the bidding period expired. My point is that you should not delay this important step; as mentioned before, the best deals do not last long. Experienced real estate investors keep a watch on the HUD market and will bid on deals consistently, so your preparation to bid on HUD listings is critical in the early stages of finding a deal.

HUD Bidding Process

The Department of Housing and Urban Development was founded in 1965. One of its primary purposes was to promote equality among homebuyers. That mission has continued today, making HUD far more inclined to work with buyers who intend to occupy the property for a minimum of a year than profit-seeking investors like you and I.

If you remember from earlier, there are two bidding periods with HUD homes: the exclusive period and the extended period.

HUD properties that are FHA insurable, which is based on their livable condition, start their time on the market as *exclusive*. This means that HUD will only accept bids from owner-occupants, non-profits, and government agencies. After an exclusive bid is accepted, the owner-occupant buyer will sign several affidavits that say that the buyer intends to occupy the property during the first year of ownership. This affidavit comes with strict warnings and an extensive penalty schedule that includes lofty fines and even threatens imprisonment for violations of this agreement. My advice is to heed this warning and occupy the property for the required time. However, many of my HUD buyers during my agent career were military personnel, so some could not occupy the house for a full year. However, as long as the buyer *intends* to occupy the property for a year, I feel confident that HUD takes no issue with unforeseen circumstances like a military relocation. Most people don't want to move in less than a year anyway, so HUD homes can be excellent for first-time home buyers looking to build some sweat equity in their home. Unfortunately, most retail buyers are looking for homes in tip-top condition. As such, perfectly viable HUD homes often languish on the market during the exclusive period. Smart investors will monitor homes during the exclusive period and prepare their bid and financing for the day after the exclusive period ends.

With this in mind, you may be thinking that HUDs in their exclusive period are of little use to a fix and flipper who intends to resell the property in ninety days. And you'd be correct. A HUD property purchased during the exclusive period will also be issued a deed restriction that will prevent the transfer of the deed for twelve months from the purchase date. I've never dealt with anyone who tried to get around this rule, but I can tell you from my experience with HUD that this restriction is taken very seriously.

If you are an investor who intends to live in your flip property, the exclusive sales period can be a major advantage to you. Investor-buyers purchase a significant percentage of HUD properties, so being able to have an edge on your investor competition may be exactly what you need to find your next deal. However, the occupancy requirement does create the challenge of promising to occupy the property for one year after closing, so it can slow your investment growth process. The investor's best bet is to monitor the progress of the property on the HUD site and know in advance when it will transfer to the next status. This date is indicated on the HUD site by the bidding period countdown shown in the details of the property.

The second buying period, if you remember, is known as the extended period. While the bidding process is fundamentally the same, this period allows investor-buyers as well as owner-occupied buyers to bid on HUD homes. The extended buying period starts immediately on the listing date on properties that require too much work to be FHA insurable. Properties that start in the exclusive period generally change to extended status after thirty days on the market. In the HUD boom era, I found a significant number of deals by tracking the listing date of exclusive-status HUD properties. By knowing the earliest date I could submit a bid as an investor, I could wait until 12:01 a.m. on the date of the extended period and have my HUD bid submitted before most investors were even aware the property was available to investors. I fondly refer to this process as "sniping" because I feel like an operative working late at night to snipe a great HUD deal while most investors are sleeping.

This is just one of the great tricks I share as a real estate investing coach. If you'd like to learn more, please contact me today by scheduling a quick zoom call with me at:

www.foreclosuredealscoach.com.

So What Now?

Did you find your HUD registered agent? If not, hop on the broker search and find one now. If your preferred agent wants to get registered but is unfamiliar with the bidding process, send them this video that will walk them through the bidding process: https://www.youtube.com/watch?v=aa7mnYw30SI. It isn't very complicated, but it is substantially different from the standard real estate contracting process, so it will help your agent to get some background in advance.

Source #3 Wholesalers

A *real estate wholesaler* is an individual or company that specializes in the facilitation of real estate transactions without actually taking ownership of the property. Instead, wholesalers act as intermediaries who identify and secure potential real estate deals and then assign or sell the rights to purchase those properties to other investors for a fee. This process is known as *real estate wholesaling* and involves several key steps:

1) Identification of opportunities: Real estate wholesalers are often skilled at identifying distressed or undervalued properties with the potential for improvement. This can include properties facing foreclosure, in need of repairs, or with motivated sellers looking for a quick sale.

2) Marketing and negotiation: Once a potential opportunity is identified, the wholesaler negotiates with the property owner to secure it at a favorable price. Effective negotiation skills are crucial in this phase, as wholesalers aim to acquire the property at a price that allows for a profitable resale or assignment.

3) Securing the property under contract: To control the property without actually buying it, the wholesaler enters into a contractual agreement with the seller. This agreement, known as a *purchase and sale agreement* or *an option contract*, gives the

wholesaler the right to buy the property at an agreed-upon price within a specified time frame.

4) Building a buyer's list: Simultaneously, wholesalers work on building a network of potential buyers or investors interested in purchasing distressed or undervalued properties. This network often includes fix-and-flip investors, landlords, or other real estate professionals looking for investment opportunities.

5) Marketing the contract: With the property under contract, the wholesaler markets the deal to their network of buyers. This involves creating a comprehensive marketing package that outlines the details of the property, the purchase price, and the terms of the deal.

6) Assignment of contract or double closing: Once a buyer is interested, the wholesaler has two primary methods to close the deal. In an assignment of contract, the wholesaler sells or assigns the contractual rights to purchase the property to the end buyer for a fee. In a double closing, the wholesaler closes on the property with the original seller and, on the same day, sells it to the end buyer.

7) Earning a fee or profit: The profit for the wholesaler comes from the difference between the contracted purchase price and the price at which they assign or sell the contract to the end buyer. This fee, sometimes referred to as the *wholesale fee*, compensates the wholesaler for their efforts in identifying and securing the deal.

8) Risks and challenges: While real estate wholesaling can be lucrative, it comes with risks and challenges. Wholesalers need to

be knowledgeable about the local real estate market, have effective negotiation skills, and understand legal and contractual obligations. Additionally, building and maintaining a reliable network of buyers is crucial for consistent success.

I have been investing in real estate for fifteen years, but in the past four years, we have ramped up our annual targets for flips. During this time, I have had the pleasure of working with some great wholesalers and some not-so-great ones. For those unfamiliar with wholesale, there are a ton of resources on wholesaling education available on YouTube. The basics of wholesaling is that the wholesaler "locks" a property up with a contract to buy it at a certain price. The wholesaler then adds a wholesale or assignment fee to the purchase price, which is basically their profit for putting together the deal. Newbie investors often lament about this assignment fee, which I've seen be as low as $2,500 and as high as $50,000, but I explain that as long as the numbers work for you as the fix and flipper, the wholesale fee is irrelevant. Don't worry about the wholesaler's profit on the deal; focus on yourself. By doing so, you will not only analyze the deal fairly, but you will also build a long-term relationship with the wholesaler. These relationships have translated into hundreds of deals for me and millions in equity. The wholesaler-to-flipper relationships I have formed have provided me with a consistent source of great deals. Though I can find deals on all of the sources I've listed, the easiest and most reliable source I currently have is definitely wholesalers.

When you join my coaching program, one of the key benefits is that I find deals for you through my network and advertising efforts. By working with a limited number of clients, I can wholesale deals to you without creating a bidding war that drives up your pricing. In essence, I become your personal wholesaler, and in the event the deal I find doesn't work within your parameters or time frame, I can simply present the deal to one of my other clients. This is very beneficial to my coaching clients because it insures a degree of exclusivity, if that's of interest to you. Check out www.foreclosuredealscoach.com to learn more and schedule a call.

Finding Wholesalers

Meeting wholesalers is easy in most areas of the country. My best source is Facebook. To find wholesalers in your local market, use my FB group trick. Simply type "(your city) real estate investment." This will bring up a list of real estate investment groups in your local area. Note that I didn't say to join retail real estate groups. Most retail real estate groups are set up and monitored by real estate agents. Though agents can be a source of deals, it is best to work with a buyer's agent to help you identify and write offers on MLS-listed houses. The reality is that most agents are not familiar enough with the wholesale market to be effective. Wholesalers are trained to scour the market for distressed and foreclosure deals and lock them up quickly. When a wholesaler offers to send you a deal, kindly accept all of the property data. A thorough data file on a potential acquisition property should include the following:

- the address of the property
- the square footage

- the bedroom/bathroom count
- the proposed closing date
- the asking price with wholesale assignment fee included, and the comparable sales

After a while, you will learn which wholesalers in your market provide useful market data to their investors and which ones are basically in the game just to make money.

Once you have established a relationship with a good wholesaler or several, it's critical to work to maintain that relationship. To do so, you must express and maintain your integrity. Many wholesalers are doing this business full time and supporting their families by wholesaling the deal to you. As such, it's important that when you say you're going to do something, including closing on a property on a specific date, you keep that commitment. As someone who focused on the wholesale side for many years, I can tell you that getting even the most motivated seller to the deal table can be hard.

As an investor-buyer, make yourself easy to work with, and wholesalers will find you by your reputation. On the other hand, if you are difficult to work with, you may find yourself blacklisted by wholesalers. This can reduce or even eliminate your deal flow in certain markets. Integrity is critical in every business, but when dealing with one of the most valuable assets people own, it's extremely important that you remain responsive to your wholesale contacts throughout the process of acquiring your investment property. Keep in mind that the wholesaler does not *have* to sell a deal to you if it's a good deal. Good deals will have multiple potential buyers. If your wholesale relationships mean you get a first look at wholesale and can decide whether to buy or pass, consider yourself fortunate and work hard to fulfill your obligations. One of my best wholesalers brought me over twenty deals in 2021 with a backend profit of over $700K. Building and maintaining solid wholesale relationships can make or break your investment career.

So What Now?

Hop on Facebook, search for your real estate *investment* groups, and start conversations. Don't be shy; wholesalers are always looking to add to their investor buyer list. Respond to requests to add to their lists, ask for details about posted properties, and message the wholesaler and let them know that you are an active investor looking for deals in your market. Make sure your FB profile "looks" the part of a professional real estate investor. Position yourself as a serious investor in your market, and the best deal might find you!

Source #4 Real Estate Agents

After fifteen years as a licensed real estate agent, I would be remiss not to mention the people who are licensed to work in my favorite industry. As an agent, I established my brand as a deal hunter. To create this brand, I had a YouTube channel called Colorado Foreclosure Deals, where, as the name indicates, I would do walkthroughs of foreclosure properties all across the state of Colorado. The work was tough, with long days of driving, video editing, and production, but I achieved my desired result.

My market still knows me as one of the leading experts in the distressed and foreclosed property space.

If you are an agent yourself, you already have access to the MLS, but as an investor, you don't want to compete with local agents; you want to partner with them. As an investor, you won't be seen as competition but as an ally. Agents often have sellers in difficult situations, and as an established local investor, you can be a resource to these agents to help solve difficult real estate issues by buying the problematic properties quickly and with minimal hassle to the seller. Some of these life issues that a seller may be facing include the following:

- death
- divorce
- tax problems
- probate
- mechanics liens

All of these issues generally cause motivated sellers to gain more benefit from selling their property than from keeping it. One of my motivated seller clients, a good friend and mentor, explained why he sold me his place for $860,000 against a solid $1.1 million valuation. He had lost his wife after a long battle with cancer. "It was easier for me at a time in my life when I needed some things to be easier." By buying his "problematic" property, I simplified his life, learned how to do a luxury house flip, and made a great friend.

I acquired my relationship-building skills as a real estate agent. Working with people who have an emotional attachment to anything can be difficult. Good real estate agents learn the power of relationships quickly. If you can show a true benefit to the clients, you will form a relationship with that agent that will provide long-term financial and personal benefits to you *and* the real estate agent.

The key to forming solid relationships with agents is to meet them. Agents are constantly doing networking events, so try to attend as many agent mixers as possible. At these events, position yourself not only as an investor, but also as an attractive, easy-to-work-with buyer. Good agents are busy people. Make it clear once you're established that you have funds available to close. Ask other agents to share their experiences working with you. Once you understand the paperwork, offer to assist them in walking through it. Don't act like you know something you don't. Agents are trained that the wholesale market is part of the proverbial "Dark Side." Educate the ones who want to be educated. Clearly explain your value proposition to the seller and then, like with your wholesale relationships, keep your integrity intact. Simply do what you say you are going to do.

Once you've established a rapport with a licensed agent, let them know that you are an active investor looking to buy great deals in your local market. Explain any specific buying criteria, but try to be as broad as possible. Agents won't remember that you only buy 3 bedroom/2 bath houses in a specific zip code, but they will remember that you are looking to buy deals in your market. Your objective is to become front of the mind in the eyes of the real estate community. The key is to incentivize your agent relationships. One of the biggest incentives you can offer your agent partners is the ability to "double end" the commission on a deal. The standard commission for buyers and seller agents is 3 percent in most markets. However, since you are not an agent and are more interested in the deal than a commission, you can offer the agent that brings you a deal the ability to take both sides of the commission.

As an agent, I can tell you that very little would excite me more as an agent than getting double my usual rate for doing the same or even less work than a standard seller listing. Most agents have experienced "double ending" a few times at best. The sheer number of buyers agents makes it very difficult to find buyers for your listings before the agent population does. Many new agents who joined the market in the last few years don't even know that double ending a deal is possible. As an investor, your objective is to open the door to a conversation about listings that may need to be underpriced in the market to sell due to condition, timeline, or other concerns. You will receive deals from the market before your competition by making yourself front of mind in your agent community. Like your relationship with wholesalers, your agent relationships need to be protected. In addition to the monetary benefits you provide to your real estate agent partners, you can also provide a unique service to their clientele. By encouraging real estate agents to tell their clients about their partnership with you as a local investor, you also build the credibility and sales volume of the agent in question.

The competitive real estate environment also provides several less tangible benefits to the agent population. For instance, my local listing agent, who is a critical member of my team, is currently ranked in second place for volume in the state of Colorado. This ranking makes her a front runner for recognition at the national level at one of the top real estate franchises. From this ranking, my agent partner can now recruit better talent, invest less in marketing due to the built-in recognition of nationally known performance, and build a following of potential buyers and sellers. Success follows success, so high producers in every field reach out to her to create new partnerships and provide business.

On the acquisition side of real estate, it's hard to beat the power of a recognized brand's marketing. When meeting with your agent partners, explain how your business and theirs are synergistic. A few solid referral partners who understand your basic broad buying criteria can significantly impact your annual deal volume and bottom line. Incentivize your agents with more than money. Offer support in a multitude of ways. The strong business minds will gravitate toward you and advocate for you as an investor in their community.

Additionally, the market correction will lead to a significant surge in wholetail deals. As prices begin to decrease, savvy people will focus their search on buying your below-market houses, in as much as it's in a condition significantly below the market value. This means you are coming across this real-world information at the perfect time. Though these buyers make up a much smaller percentage of the market overall, their skill and desire to trade the real estate market for increasing return on investment will be insatiable. No investor can resist a good deal, especially when it's offered by a local investor they have worked with. Create a synergy with your local real estate community early and often. For many top-tier real estate investors, this deal channel can prove to be the only one you need to create a consistent deal flow.

Mindset

I hope this section has helped you overcome any limiting beliefs about finding deals in your local market. As your Foreclosure Deals Coach, the challenge that I help most people overcome is the myth that there are no deals in a local market. The reality is that there are deals in *every* market.

Finding your next deal is simply the beginning of your investment journey. Like a dog chasing a car, many newbie investors chase deals with absolutely no idea what to do if they catch one. If this describes you, don't worry.

The reality of being a professional deal hunter is that it is not the most difficult part of the process. Still, due to the extensive amount of misinformation in the marketplace, it is certainly the primary barrier of entry for most wanna-be deal hunters.

In the next chapter we will discuss what to do after you've found a deal by discussing the true art of the deal, which is **figuring** if it's actually a good deal through effective deal analysis.

CHAPTER 4

Deal Analysis

In the dynamic realm of real estate investing, the ability to conduct effective foreclosure deal analysis is a cornerstone for success. The process involves a meticulous examination of distressed properties to determine their investment potential. In this chapter, we will delve into the key steps and considerations for mastering foreclosure deal analysis.

In the previous chapter we discussed how to find a foreclosure deal. This is where many of my coaching clients fail, because they don't think there are any deals in their market or they don't know where to look for deals. Once how to locate the deals available in every market, many overconfident investors take the initial step and do their first deal, many times without understanding the next and arguably more important step of doing proper deal analysis.

There are countless statistics (aka educated guesses) on the percentage of new investors that lose money on their deals. One statistic suggests that up to 80 percent of newbie investors lose money on their first investment deal. While there are far too many factors to really determine this number with certainty, I can say that after speaking with hundreds of investors about their first deal, I think 80 percent may actually be a low estimate. People who have both the capital and the courage to do a deal without guidance are rare, but a very large percentage of people who take the leap of faith to do a deal end up on the losing end. To understand why that is, you have to first understand the complexity of doing deal analysis. Right after you go under contract on a foreclosure deal, there will be immense pressure to close and fund that deal. This pressure will come from a variety of sources, including the motivated seller who wants to get rid of a problematic property; the agent representing that seller, because they are eager to get paid their commission; the wholesaler who put the deal together; the seller's bank, who is working on the foreclosure; the hard money lender, who has limited access to the funds needed for closing; the title company, who has to prepare the documents for the closing, which are only valid for limited period of time; the contractor, who wants to get started on the work; and list of others who may be involved in the transaction. Doing deal analysis in a low-stress environment is hard enough, but having a group of people pressuring you to make a decision can make the decision process infinitely more difficult. As a result, I see many new investors succumb to the pressure under a "fail forward fast" mindset, which I generally support. However, with the high capital requirements in real estate investing, one significant failure can wipe out such a significant portion of your investment capital that it often takes new investors years to recover. As such, I teach my clients the importance of efficient, quick, and effective deal analysis.

Before diving into analysis, it's crucial to grasp the various stages of foreclosure. From pre-foreclosure and auction to postforeclosure or real estate owned (REO), each stage presents unique challenges and opportunities. Knowing the intricacies of the foreclosure process sets the foundation for effective analysis.

Financial Analysis

It is critical to perform a comprehensive financial analysis to evaluate investment viability. This includes assessing the property's current market value, potential repair costs, and outstanding liens or encumbrances. Accurate financial projections are essential for determining the potential return on investment (ROI).

Due Diligence on Property Conditions

Conduct a thorough examination of the property's physical condition. This involves on-site inspections, obtaining professional property inspections, and estimating repair costs. Accurate assessments ensure that the true cost of rehabilitation is factored into the overall investment. Many of the problems with a foreclosure are not visible without removing parts of the property, so knowing the hard costs of certain repairs is important to allow for some wiggle room in the total repair costs.

Title Search and Legal Considerations

A meticulous title search is imperative to uncover any outstanding liens, back taxes, or legal issues associated with the property. Engage a qualified title company to ensure a clear title, protecting you from unforeseen legal complications. I see investors glaze over the title documents far too often because they tend to be long and can be hard to decipher, so using an investor-friendly title company is important to ensure you aren't buying a home with both physical deficiencies and title deficiencies.

Analyzing Comparable Sales

Examine recent comparable sales (comps) in the area to gauge the property's market value. Consider factors such as location, size, condition, and amenities. This comparative analysis aids in setting a competitive and realistic purchase price. Accessing comparable sold properties was once limited to licensed real estate agents, but today tools like www.fdcdealcheck.com allow you to include comparable sales in your analysis as well as a significant number of other variables that go into a profitable foreclosure flip.

Evaluating Neighborhood and Market Trends

Understanding the neighborhood and broader market trends is vital. Factors such as job growth, local development projects, and economic indicators influence the property's long-term potential. A thriving neighborhood contributes to property appreciation over time, while a declining neighborhood or overall market can leave you owning a property for longer than intended. Neighborhood trend analysis will allow you to properly determine your exit asking price based on the trend. While most markets allow the use of six months of comparable analysis, recent market shifts have dropped analysis to as little as thirty days of neighborhood market trend analysis, which significantly reduces the available data and makes analysis both more difficult and more subjective.

Financial Exit Strategies

Before finalizing a deal, develop clear exit strategies. Whether it's fixing and flipping, renting, or selling to another investor, having well-defined exit plans ensures flexibility and adaptability in changing market conditions. I generally recommend that my clients start with a fix-and-flip exit strategy for their first deal with me. This allows them to recover their initial investment in the coaching and the investment property within 90 to 120 days. By doing so, coaching clients gain both the confidence and capital needed quickly to advance their investing career.

Networking and Professional Advice

Engage with professionals in the industry, including real estate agents, contractors, and attorneys. Networking provides valuable insights, and seeking professional advice ensures that legal, financial, and logistical aspects are appropriately addressed. You've probably heard the saying that your network is your net worth. By forming a team of experienced professionals around you, you will be able to increase both the volume and the profitability of your investment deals.

Risk Mitigation

Every real estate investment carries inherent risks. Identify potential challenges and develop mitigation strategies. Consider market volatility, economic downturns, and unforeseen repairs. A well-prepared investor is better equipped to navigate challenges. A better-prepared investor understands the importance of bringing professional guidance to the table when starting their investment journey.

I certainly would not be the real estate investor I am today without having found and retained my coach so many years ago, and I am certain that everyone in this industry can benefit from getting the professional guidance offered by effective real estate investment coaching.

Foreclosure deal analysis is both an art and a science. It requires a keen understanding of market dynamics, property conditions, legal intricacies, and financial considerations. Mastering this skill empowers investors to identify lucrative opportunities, make informed decisions, and navigate the complexities of distressed property investments.

As you embark on your journey into foreclosure deal analysis, remember that each property is unique, and adaptability is key to success in the ever-evolving landscape of real estate investing. If this seems like a lot to figure out on your own, it's because it is. But once you learn and understand how to do effective foreclosure deal analysis, it will feel much like owning a machine that can print money. There are deals everywhere, but not all foreclosures are deals, and not all deals are foreclosures.

Work to become effective at deal analysis, and you will be able to quickly and effectively do deal analysis on any foreclosure deal in the country. With the wave of foreclosures poised to hit the market in coming years, now is an excellent time to learn and master this invaluable skill.

On the surface, deal analysis will seem very complicated to a new investor. How do you determine the value when there are so many variables to work with? When you start to consider floor plan, location, square footage, age of windows, appliances, neighborhood trends, school district, etc., it is easy to see why investors can become overwhelmed. To simplify all of the variables, I teach my investors a very simple three-number analysis to make deal analysis faster and easier.

My three-number system will allow you to evaluate deals in any area and make a quick decision on whether to do a full analysis on the deal or to pass on it immediately.

The three-number system is as follows:

The After Repaired Value (ARV) - (Acquisition Price + Rehab Price) will help you determine your gross profit on the deal.

From there we take the Gross Profit and divide it by 2 to determine the Potential Gross Profit.

For my clients in my local market, we find deals that show a minimum of $50,000 in gross profit, resulting in a $25,000 profit for fix-and-flip deals using this formula. While markets have some variation in different parts of the country, I have found this formula to be effective in quickly determining potential gross and net profit on deals.

Once you have determined that the gross profit on a deal you are evaluating is sufficient, the next step is to use tools like Dealcheck.io to enter all of the other variables, including cost of funds, transaction costs, and itemized rehab estimates to dial in your numbers for accuracy.

Chapter Conclusion

Deal analysis is both an art and a science, and like any skill, it is developed over time. When you first start learning this skill, you should expect and budget for one to two hours to complete a deal analysis. Over time I have been able to get this time frame to thirty minutes or less, but it has taken years of consistent practice and the addition of deal analysis tools like Dealcheck.io.

Deal analysis is not covered on reality TV series because there is nothing fun or exciting about the process. When I'm coaching my clients, I help them analyze the deals we do together in the same manner that my real estate investment coach did for me many years ago. Like learning to day trade stock, the best way to learn deal analysis is on "practice deals" that you aren't actually looking to buy. This practice is tedious, but removing the emotion from your deal analysis by "paper trading" with practice properties in the Dealcheck.io tool (www.fdcdealcheck.com) will build your confidence as a foreclosure investor faster and more effectively than reading books or taking courses on real estate investing. Get started today and develop the habit of analyzing deals as often as possible.

CHAPTER 5

NAVIGATING FORECLOSURE DEAL FUNDING

Hard Money vs. Conventional Lending vs. Private Money

In the dynamic world of real estate investing, funding is the lifeblood of successful transactions. When it comes to foreclosure deals, investors often explore various financing options to leverage their capital effectively. In this chapter, we'll delve into the key considerations of utilizing hard money, conventional lending, and private money for funding foreclosure deals. Because every financing situation is fundamentally different, I'm going to use this chapter to give you a quick set of pros and cons to consider each of the three primary sources of financing I use to fund my deals and the deals of my clients, so you can best determine which financing option is best for you and the deal you are working on.

1. Hard Money Lending:

Pros:

- Speed and flexibility: Hard money lenders are known for their quick approval processes, making them ideal for time-sensitive foreclosure deals.
- Asset-based lending: Approval is primarily based on the value of the property rather than the borrower's

creditworthiness, making it accessible for investors with less-than-stellar credit.

- Accessibility: Hard money lenders are often more open to funding deals that may be considered too risky by traditional lenders.

Cons:

- High costs: Hard money loans typically come with higher interest rates and fees than conventional loans.
- Shorter terms: Hard money loans are usually short-term, requiring prompt repayment or refinancing.
- Stringent terms: Lenders may impose strict terms, and failure to meet them could result in severe consequences.

2. Conventional Lending:

Pros:

- Lower interest rates: Conventional loans generally offer lower interest rates compared to hard money loans.
- Longer terms: Conventional mortgages often come with longer repayment terms, providing investors with greater flexibility.
- Regulatory protection: Conventional lenders adhere to strict regulations, providing borrowers with a level of consumer protection.

Cons:

- Stringent approval criteria: Conventional lenders place a strong emphasis on the borrower's creditworthiness, financial stability, and income.
- Slower approval process: Conventional loans may involve a more extended approval process, which can be a disadvantage in competitive real estate markets.
- Property condition requirements: Conventional lenders may have strict property condition standards, limiting the types of distressed properties they are willing to finance.

3. Private Money:

Pros:

- Flexibility: Private money lenders often offer flexible terms and repayment schedules negotiated directly between the borrower and lender.
- Relationship-based: Transactions with private lenders can be more personalized and based on individual relationships.
- Quick approval: Similar to hard money lenders, private money lenders may offer quicker approval processes.

Cons:

- Varied terms: Terms can vary widely based on the specific arrangement between the borrower and the private lender.

- Limited accessibility: Access to private money often depends on personal relationships or networks.
- Risk of strained relationships: When using money from friends or family, there's a potential risk of straining personal relationships if the investment doesn't go as planned.

Choosing the Right Funding Source

The decision between hard money, conventional lending, and private money depends on various factors, including the investor's financial situation, the urgency of the deal, and the level of risk tolerance. Investors should carefully consider the terms, costs, and potential risks associated with each financing option.

Successful funding of foreclosure deals is a critical aspect of real estate investing. Each financing option—hard money, conventional lending, and private money—comes with its own set of advantages and disadvantages. By understanding the unique characteristics of each option and aligning them with individual investment goals and circumstances, investors can make informed decisions that maximize returns and mitigate risks in the competitive landscape of foreclosure deals.

CHAPTER 6

General Contractor vs. Project Manager in Foreclosure Deals

As a real estate investor diving into a foreclosure deal, know that the rehabilitation or fixing phase is a critical juncture that demands effective management and execution. In this chapter, we will explore the roles of a general contractor and a project manager, comparing their contributions, strengths, and potential considerations in the context of foreclosure property renovations.

Similar to the last chapter, this chapter gives a wide variety of options to consider when working through the process of fixing your deal. In the end, your decision will come down to the most cost-effective way to get your deal back to salable condition.

While many investors immediately assume that hiring a general contractor is the best choice for completing the remodeling process, in my experience, general contractors are generally too expensive to be used on most projects.

What general contractors offer is the relationships they have formed with subcontractors they can mark up to make a profit. As the costs of materials and labor have risen to unprecedented levels in the last few years, it is difficult to make a profit with the added cost of a general contractor.

Like with any home remodeling project, the ability to manage your own fix-and-flip project will allow you to find and complete profitable deals consistently.

Now, it is important to note that the role of real estate investor is not a construction-based role. If you are the handy type and can do some of the basic construction work yourself, it will definitely increase your overall profitability on a deal due to reduced labor costs, but that savings usually comes at the expense of time. In the foreclosure investment business, time is literally money. While you may save money by swinging a hammer on your fix-and-flip project, if you are using hard money, that savings will generally be offset by an increased cost of funds due to the longer use of the funds, in addition to the opportunity cost of being able to do fewer deals due to the longer timeframe of each deal. My objective here is to ensure that you understand that while many investors, including me, started in the foreclosure investment business by doing a lot of the construction work themselves, this is, at best, a short solution only to be used in the early stages of your investing career.

Your objective is to build an investment company that allows you to build a portfolio. Wealthy investors rarely do manual labor in the long-term pursuit of building wealth. If you already have a lot of experience and knowledge in the construction industry, then you are at a significant advantage in this space. However, this knowledge is not required to be successful in this industry. The skill set you will require to complete your flip will be project management and leadership skills.

When my wife and I first started our flipping business, we did what I refer to as a "point and click" rehab model. Basically, we would walk through the flips and point out the deficiencies, and then we would hire the appropriate subcontractors to complete the work. While sheer determination, persistence, and a lot of hard work allowed us to make a lot of progress, over time I learned the importance of proper project planning before we started our remodels.

Today, the pre-construction can take up to half the time of the actual construction timeline. By planning your project in advance, you can reduce your costs and timeframes by a substantial margin.

Once you have a proper pre-construction process, you can decide on the appropriate construction team for your project.

The three documents required to plan your project are the scope of work, the materials takeoff list, and the labor estimate. Additionally, many investors get a 3D rendering of their project to provide a visual representation to their construction team. Construction software platforms like Cedreo (www.cedreo.com) and Cost Certified (www.costcertfied.com) will help you to build your scope of work, materials takeoff list, and labor estimates quickly to help you determine the right team for your project.

Scope of Work

A remodeling scope of work (SOW) is a document that outlines the specific details and requirements of a remodeling project. It serves as a roadmap for the remodeling contractor and helps ensure that both the client's expectations and the contractor's responsibilities are clearly defined. Here are the key elements typically included in a remodeling scope of work:

- Project overview:
  - Brief description of the remodeling project, its purpose, and objectives.
  - Identification of the client and any relevant stakeholders.

- Project goals:
  - Clearly defined goals and objectives of the remodeling project.
  - Specific outcomes or improvements expected upon project completion.

- Scope of services:
  - Detailed list of the remodeling tasks to be performed by the contractor.
  - Specifications for materials, finishes, and construction methods.

- Project area and description:
  - Description of the specific areas or rooms to be remodeled.
  - Any existing structures, fixtures, or features that will be affected.

- Design and layout:

  o Plans and drawings specifying the proposed changes to the existing layout.

  o Details on any architectural or design elements to be incorporated.

- Demolition and construction:

  o Description of demolition work, if applicable.

  o Construction details, including the installation of new elements or features.

- Materials and finishes:

  o Specifications for all materials, finishes, and fixtures to be used.

  o Brand names, model numbers, and any specific requirements.

- Permits and approvals:

  o Identification of required permits and approvals.

  o Responsibility for obtaining necessary permissions from local authorities.

- Timeline and schedule:

  o Clear timelines for project commencement, milestones, and completion.

  o Coordination with the client regarding any specific timing requirements.

- Site conditions:

  o Evaluation of existing site conditions and any potential challenges.

  o Measures to address issues such as structural concerns or environmental factors.

- Utilities and services:

  o Coordination with utility providers for any necessary disconnections or reconnections.

  o Temporary services required during the remodeling process.

- Health and safety measures:

  o Safety protocols for both workers and occupants during the remodeling.

  o Compliance with occupational health and safety regulations.

- Waste management:

  o Procedures for handling and disposing of construction waste.

  o Recycling or disposal methods in accordance with local regulations.

- Payment terms:

  o Clearly defined payment milestones, terms, and conditions.

  o Procedures for handling change orders and additional work.

- Communication protocols:

  o   Guidelines for regular project updates and communication channels.

  o   Contact information for key project personnel.

- Completion and acceptance criteria:

  o   Criteria that must be met for the client to accept the completed remodeling.

  o   Punch list items for final inspections and corrections.

- Contractual terms and conditions:

  o   Legal and contractual obligations of both parties.

  o   Signatures of authorized representatives to signify agreement and acceptance.

A well-drafted remodeling scope of work ensures that both the client and the contractor have a clear understanding of the project's parameters, minimizing the risk of misunderstandings and disputes and facilitating a successful remodeling project.

Materials Takeoff

A materials takeoff (often abbreviated as "take-off" or "BOM" for *bill of materials*) list is a detailed list of all the materials and quantities needed for a construction project. It serves as a critical component in project estimation, budgeting, and procurement. For remodeling construction, a materials takeoff list includes the specific materials required for the remodeling project. Here's an explanation of the key elements typically found in a Materials Takeoff List for remodeling:

- Project information:
  - Project name, location, and date of the takeoff.
  - Identification of the person or entity performing the takeoff.
- Area or room breakdown:
  - Division of the project into specific areas or rooms.
  - Identification of materials needed for each area or room.
- Demolition materials:
  - List of materials required for demolition, if applicable. This may include tools, protective gear, and disposal containers.
- Structural materials:
  - Materials needed for any structural modifications or additions, for example, framing lumber, beams, and structural fasteners.
- Finish materials:
  - Materials for finishing surfaces, such as walls, floors, and ceilings. This may include drywall, flooring materials, and ceiling finishes.
- Plumbing materials:
  - Items required for plumbing modifications or installations. Examples include pipes, fittings, fixtures, and water heaters.

- Electrical materials:
  - Materials needed for electrical work, such as wiring, outlets, switches, and fixtures.
- HVAC materials:
  - Materials required for heating, ventilation, and air conditioning modifications. This may include ductwork, vents, and HVAC units.
- Cabinetry and millwork:
  - Materials for custom cabinetry or millwork. Includes wood, hardware, and finishing materials.
- Paint and finishes:
  - List of paints, primers, and finishes required for the project.
  - Differentiate between interior and exterior finishes as needed.
- Doors and windows:
  - Materials for doors and windows, including frames, glass, and hardware.
  - Specify sizes and types for each.
- Fixtures and accessories:
  - Include items like faucets, sinks, lighting fixtures, and other accessories.
  - Specify styles, finishes, and quantities.

- Hardware and fasteners:

  o List of screws, nails, bolts, and other fasteners.

  o Include any specialized hardware needed for the project.

- Insulation and weatherproofing:

  o Materials for insulation and weatherproofing.

  o Specify types and quantities for walls, roofs, and other relevant areas.

- Miscellaneous supplies:

  o Any additional supplies or tools required for the project.

  o This may include adhesives, sealants, and cleaning materials.

- Contingency:

  o Allowance for unexpected changes or additional materials.

  o Typically calculated as a percentage of the total material cost.

- Total quantities and costs:

  o Summarize the quantities and costs for each category and for the overall project.

  o Provide a total cost estimate based on the materials listed.

Creating a comprehensive materials takeoff list for remodeling construction is essential for accurate budgeting, procurement planning, and ensuring that all necessary materials are accounted for during the project. It also serves as a valuable reference throughout the construction process.

Labor Estimate List

A labor estimate list for a remodeling construction project outlines the anticipated labor requirements and associated costs for completing specific tasks within the project. This list is a crucial component of project planning and budgeting, helping contractors and project managers allocate resources effectively. Here's an explanation of the key elements typically included in a labor estimate list for remodeling construction:

- Project information:
    - Project name, location, and date of the estimate.
    - Identification of the person or entity preparing the estimate.

- Scope of work:
    - A brief description of the remodeling project's scope of work.
    - Reference to the detailed scope of work document for more information.

- Task breakdown:
    - Division of the project into specific tasks or activities.
    - Identification of the labor required for each task.

- Demolition labor:

  o Estimate of labor hours needed for demolition activities.

  o Include tasks such as removal of existing structures, walls, or finishes.

- Structural work:

  o Labor estimate for any structural modifications or additions. Tasks may include framing, installation of beams, and other structural work.

- Finish work:

  o Estimate of labor hours for finishing surfaces, such as drywall installation and finishing.

  o Include any special finishes or detailing.

- Plumbing labor:

  o Labor estimate for plumbing modifications or installations. Tasks may include pipe installation, fixture installation, and connections.

- Electrical labor:

  o Estimate of labor hours for electrical work, including wiring and installation of outlets and switches.

  o Specify if specialized electrical tasks are required.

- HVAC labor:

  o Estimate of labor hours for heating, ventilation, and air conditioning work.

- o Include tasks related to ductwork, system installation, and testing.

- Cabinetry and millwork installation:

  - o Labor estimate for the installation of custom cabinetry and millwork.
  - o Specify tasks related to fabrication, installation, and finishing.

- Painting and finishing labor:

  - o Estimate of labor hours for painting and finishing surfaces.
  - o Include any surface preparation work.

- Door and window installation:

  - o Labor estimate for the installation of doors and windows.
  - o Specify tasks related to framing, installation, and finishing.

- Fixture and accessory installation:

  - o Estimate of labor hours for installing fixtures and accessories.
  - o Include tasks such as installing faucets, sinks, lighting fixtures, and other accessories.

- Hardware installation:

  - o Estimate of labor hours for installing hardware.
  - o Include tasks such as installing door handles, locks, and other hardware.

- Insulation and weatherproofing labor:
  - o Estimate of labor hours for installing insulation and weatherproofing materials.
  - o Specify tasks related to insulation placement and sealing.
- Clean-up and final touches:
  - o Estimate of labor hours for cleaning up the site and completing final touches.
  - o Include tasks such as removal of debris and final inspections.
- Contingency:
  - o Allowance for unexpected labor requirements. Typically calculated as a percentage of the total labor cost.
- Total labor hours and costs:
  - o Summarize the labor hours and costs for each task and for the overall project.
  - o Provide a total labor cost estimate based on the labor hours and rates.

Creating a detailed labor estimate list is crucial for accurate project budgeting, resource allocation, and overall project management. It helps ensure that the necessary labor is accounted for, reducing the risk of cost overruns and delays. Additionally, it serves as a valuable reference throughout the construction process.

Once you have successfully created the three data sheets needed to start your remodeling project, the depth of the remodeling project will allow you to decide whether to manage the project yourself, hire a project manager, or, in extreme cases, hire a general contractor to complete your project. The following section will give you the pros and cons of a general contractor versus a project manager.

**1. The Role of a General Contractor:

Pros:

- Construction expertise: General contractors (GCs) are seasoned professionals with expertise in various construction trades. They oversee the day-to-day construction activities and ensure the work meets industry standards.
- Subcontractor management: GCs manage subcontractors, ensuring that the right professionals handle specialized tasks such as plumbing, electrical work, and carpentry.
- Material procurement: They handle the sourcing and procurement of construction materials, leveraging their industry connections for cost-effective and quality supplies.

Cons:

- Cost: General contractors often charge a percentage of the total project cost as their fee, which can add a significant expense to the rehabilitation budget.

- Limited oversight: Depending on their workload, GCs may manage multiple projects simultaneously, potentially leading to reduced oversight and attention to detail.

**2. The Role of a Project Manager:

Pros:

- Holistic project oversight: Project managers (PMs) take a comprehensive approach, overseeing all aspects of the project, including budgeting, scheduling, and quality control.
- Vendor coordination: PMs coordinate and manage vendors and subcontractors, ensuring seamless communication and collaboration among all project participants.
- Budget management: They play a crucial role in budgeting, helping investors make informed decisions and avoid cost overruns through careful planning and tracking.
- Risk mitigation: Project managers are adept at identifying potential risks and developing strategies to mitigate them, contributing to smoother project execution.

Cons:

- May require a higher fee: Depending on their level of expertise and the scope of the project, PMs may charge higher fees for their comprehensive services.

- Limited expertise in specific trades: While PMs have a broad understanding of construction projects, they may lack the specialized knowledge of specific trades compared to a general contractor.

Choosing Between a General Contractor and a Project Manager

The decision between a general contractor and a project manager hinges on the specific needs and preferences of the investor. Here are some considerations:

- Project manager complexity: For more straightforward projects with well-defined scopes, a project manager may be sufficient. For complex renovations requiring meticulous planning, a general contractor may provide more comprehensive oversight.

- Budget constraints: Investors with budget constraints may lean toward a general contractor, as they often charge a percentage fee, while project managers may require a higher upfront fee.

- Investor involvement: Some investors prefer more hands-on involvement in the project, and a general contractor might suit their needs. Investors seeking a more hands-off approach and comprehensive project oversight may opt for a project manager.

Conclusion

The choice between a general contractor and a project manager is a crucial decision in the rehabilitation phase of a foreclosure deal. Investors should carefully evaluate their project's scope and budget, as well as their own preferences in terms of involvement and oversight. Whether opting for the expertise of a general contractor or the comprehensive management of a project manager, successful rehabilitation is contingent on effective communication, collaboration, and a shared commitment to realizing the full potential of the investment property.

CHAPTER 7

FLIPPING A FORECLOSURE DEAL

Cost-Effective Strategies for Success

Flipping a foreclosure deal requires a strategic approach to maximizing profits while minimizing transaction costs. In this chapter, we will explore three key aspects of the flipping process: utilizing a hold-open title policy to reduce transaction costs, preparing the property for sale, and leveraging a discount agent to list the property.

**1. Hold Open Title Policy for Cost Reduction

Understanding Hold-Open Title Policies

A hold-open title policy is a title insurance policy that remains in effect for an extended period, accommodating the time needed to buy, renovate, and sell a property. This can be particularly beneficial in foreclosure deals, where the timeline for acquisition and resale may be more unpredictable.

Reducing Transaction Costs

By utilizing a hold-open title policy, investors can potentially reduce transaction costs associated with obtaining a new title insurance policy for each transaction phase.

This policy streamlines the process and minimizes the need for additional title searches and insurance, offering a cost-effective solution for investors engaged in the quick turnover of properties.

**2. Preparing the Property for Sale

Curated Renovations

Effective property preparation involves strategic renovations that enhance the property's appeal without unnecessary expenses. Focus on essential repairs and cosmetic upgrades that align with market demands.

Professional Staging

Consider professional staging to showcase the property's potential. Staged homes often attract more buyers and can command higher prices. This initial investment can yield substantial returns in terms of the property's perceived value.

Strategic Marketing Materials

Create high-quality marketing materials, including professional photographs, virtual tours, and compelling property descriptions. An enticing online presence can attract a broader audience and generate more interest in the property.

**3. Using a Discount Agent to List the Property for Sale

Benefits of Discount Agents

Discount real estate agents offer reduced commission rates compared to traditional agents, providing an opportunity to cut selling costs. While they may offer a discounted service, many are experienced professionals with the skills needed to effectively market and sell properties.

Interviewing Potential Agents

When selecting a discount agent, conduct thorough interviews to ensure they understand your goals and have experience in selling properties similar to yours. Assess their marketing strategies, negotiation skills, and knowledge of the local market.

Negotiating Commission Rates

Negotiate commission rates with the agent upfront. While discount agents may offer lower rates, it's essential to strike a balance that still motivates them to actively market and sell the property. In the markets I work in, I have negotiated an incredible listing commission discount for my clients, allowing them to maximize their profitability while still working with an agent that is effective at marketing and selling their deal.

Conclusion

Flipping a foreclosure deal successfully involves a combination of strategic financial decisions, effective property preparation, and savvy marketing. Utilizing a hold-open title policy can streamline the transaction process and reduce costs, while a carefully prepared property can attract a higher number of potential buyers. Leveraging a discount agent further contributes to cost savings without compromising the quality of the selling process. By combining these strategies, investors can enhance their profitability and navigate the challenges of flipping foreclosure deals with confidence.

Chapter 8

The Next Steps on Your Foreclosure-Flipping Journey

You now know all the basics for starting your foreclosure-flipping journey, from finding great deals on homes, securing funding, and managing renovations to optimizing the selling process for the best results. Simple right?

If you are like most people, yes, this all sounds simple on the surface, and you know this book has just given you a clear and straightforward roadmap for navigating your journey through this process. You feel motivated and inspired to tackle the process and start seeing those big paydays because I have given you the confidence to do it with the step-by-step guidance I have provided.

However, you may also realize that this is a *huge* project, which will require a lot of cash and has the risk of leaving you with little to no profit—or worse, an actual negative ROI—if not done correctly.

I'm not trying to burst your bubble here, but that is how most people feel—a little apprehensive or even overwhelmed—when they do their first flip or two. And most flippers, unless they are extremely lucky or have a friend or family member to help them along the way, do actually end up losing some money on those first few flips and not progressing as fast as they'd like, though they do learn some good lessons along the way.

But what if I told you there is a much easier way to do your first flip? What if you could have your own personal guide, someone who has done this hundreds of times and has the process down to a science, to help you along the way and make sure you don't make any of those big mistakes?

What if you could cut down your learning curve and possibly still make a larger profit than you normally would on your first try, just because you have a trusted advisor looking out for you, watching over your shoulder step-by-step, and steering you away from the pitfalls you will undoubtedly encounter during your first flip?

And what if you knew that once you did this flip, you would have even more confidence to do the next flip, along with a nice pot of cash to help you get started, because you made the right decisions, know what to look out for, and have a solid knowledge base to use on the next flip and all the flips after?

All those things and so much more are exactly what you will experience when you work with a knowledgeable coach or mentor on your foreclosure-flipping journey. I know that I wouldn't be where I am right now without the mentors, partners, and network I had throughout my real estate investment career, and now I'd like to offer all my years of experience and knowledge to you.

It's true, I have already given you all you need to know to get started on your own without me. But I can guarantee that with my help, the process will be less stressful, profitable, and maybe even fun!

If you think you'd like a helping hand to get you started on your first foreclosure flip, to hold you accountable and see you through from the purchase to the closing of your first flip, I invite you to take the next step in your journey by scheduling a coaching assessment call with me. This one-on-one session will provide an opportunity for us to explore your aspirations, evaluate your current approach to real estate investing, and chart a personalized path forward.

During our coaching assessment call, we'll delve into your specific circumstances, address any questions you may have, and determine if coaching is the right fit for you. Whether you're a seasoned investor seeking to refine your strategies or a newcomer eager to embark on your first foreclosure-flipping venture, personalized coaching can be the catalyst that propels you toward success.

If you're ready to experience schedule your FREE coaching assessment call, please visit ForeclosureDealsCoach.com and click the link to schedule a call. Let's work together to turn your real estate ambitions into tangible, profitable results.

Remember, the path to foreclosure flipping success is a dynamic and evolving journey, and having a seasoned guide by your side can make all the difference. I look forward to the opportunity to support you on your way to achieving your real estate investment goals. Wishing you prosperity and success in your foreclosure-flipping ventures!

Donny Coram
Real Estate Investor and Coach

Conclusion

I sincerely hope this e-book has provided you with enough information and guidance to start your investing journey. If you feel this was exactly the information you needed to get started, let me know by posting in my Facebook group or shooting me an email at donny@traccap.com. Hearing your story will give me the additional inspiration I need to help you and others achieve the three freedoms that I believe real estate investing is uniquely qualified to provide: financial, location, and time freedom. If this is all you need to start your journey, then it was my honor to have been a part of it.

However, years of experience with new and experienced investors have taught me that this is usually just enough information to whet your appetite. If you have read this beginning phase and want to learn the next step, I'd be honored to be considered as your real estate coach.

Please note: I said coach, not mentor. The difference is that I am interested in both providing you the info you need to become excited about real estate investing *and* being your accountability partner to help you actually get a deal done. If that's what you're looking for, I'd like to connect with you ASAP and jumpstarting your process to **finding**, **funding**, **fixing**, and **flipping** your first or next deal.

Please click on the link to schedule your coaching call and see if we are a good fit. Not only will you have access to my support and years of experience, but you can also connect with my Facebook support group as well as my private funding company, Traction Capital, which I so named because of my overwhelming desire to help real estate entrepreneurs like your gain the traction they need to stop spinning their wheels and start changing their lives.

If that sounds like you, I leave you with these parting words:

Don't buy a HOUSE buy a DEAL!!

Www.foreclosuredealscoach.com

NOTES

NOTES

NOTES

www.ingramcontent.com/pod-product-compliance
Lightning Source LLC
Chambersburg PA
CBHW072331290526
45794CB00002B/828